OWLS

BY **GAIL GIBBONS**

Holiday House / New York

To Dr. Curchin

Copyright © 2005 by Gail Gibbons
All Rights Reserved
Printed in the United States of America
www.holidayhouse.com
First Edition
1 3 5 7 9 10 8 6 4 2

Library of Congress Cataloging-in-Publication Data
Gibbons, Gail.   Owls / Gail Gibbons.—1 st ed.   p. cm.
ISBN 0-8234-1880-4
1. Owls—Juvenile literature. I. Title.
QL696.S8G53 2005 598.9'7—dc22
2004048225

Special thanks to
Barbara Allen Loucks,
Research Scientist,
New York State Department
of Environmental Conservation

On silent wings a bird swoops down in the moonlight.

The bird is an owl. Using its powerful claws, it grabs
a field mouse.

The word RAPTOR comes from the Latin word *rapere*, meaning "to grab or seize by force."

GREAT HORNED OWL

CLAWS called TALONS

The word OWL comes from the Old English word *ule*, meaning "to howl." This refers to the sound owls make.

Owls are raptors. Raptors are birds of prey, meaning they are hunters that eat meat. They grab their prey with claws, called talons, that are very sharp.

OWLS OF NORTH AMERICA

VERMICULATED OWL
(ver·MICK·u·late·ed)

FLAMMULATED OWL
(FLAM·u·late·ed)

SAW-WHET OWL
(SAW·wet)

WESTERN
SCREECH OWL

EASTERN
SCREECH OWL

MOUNTAIN
PYGMY-OWL

ELF OWL

WHISKERED
SCREECH OWL

FERRUGINOUS OWL
(fur·RU·ja·ness)

NORTHERN
PYGMY-OWL

BURROWING OWL

Most scientists believe there are about 140 different kinds of owls living around the world. They live on every continent except Antarctica. It is believed that there are 21 different kinds of owls living in North America.

The smallest owl, the elf owl, is 5 inches (12.5 cm) long from the top of its head to the tip of its tail. The largest owl, the great gray owl, is 33 inches (82.5 cm) long.

EASTERN SCREECH OWLS

Some owls have EAR TUFTS

CROWN

EARS

EYES

NECK

BACK

FACIAL DISKS

WINGS

BEAK

THROAT

BREAST

BELLY

TOES

FEET

CLAWS called TALONS

LEG

TAIL FEATHERS

Most owls have the same basic characteristics. The male is usually a little smaller than the female.

ROUND
FACIAL DISKS

BARRED
OWL

HEART-SHAPED
FACIAL DISKS

BARN OWL

There are two different types of owls. Owls with round facial disks are STRIGIDAE (STRI·juh·dee) owls. Owls with heart-shaped facial disks are TYTONIDAE (tie·TON·ih·dee) owls.

SHORT-EARED OWLS

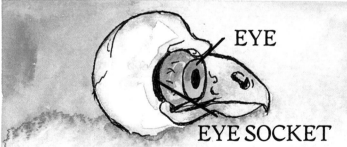

EYE

EYE SOCKET

A thick eyelid, the NICTITATING (NICK·tih·tate·ing) MEMBRANE, protects and keeps the eye clean.

The eyes of an owl cannot move in their eye sockets to watch for prey. Instead, owls have flexible necks that can twist almost completely around. They can even turn their heads upside down.

BOREAL OWL

Owls that hunt at night
are NOCTURNAL (knock·TURN·ul).

Most owls hunt at night. Day or night, they can see much better than people.

EYES AND EARS

SAW-WHET OWL

DAYLIGHT

NIGHT

Owls have very large eyes. Owls can change the focus of their eyes very rapidly and see great distances. At night the pupils of their eyes get big. This allows more light to enter into their eyes, giving them unusually good vision in the dark.

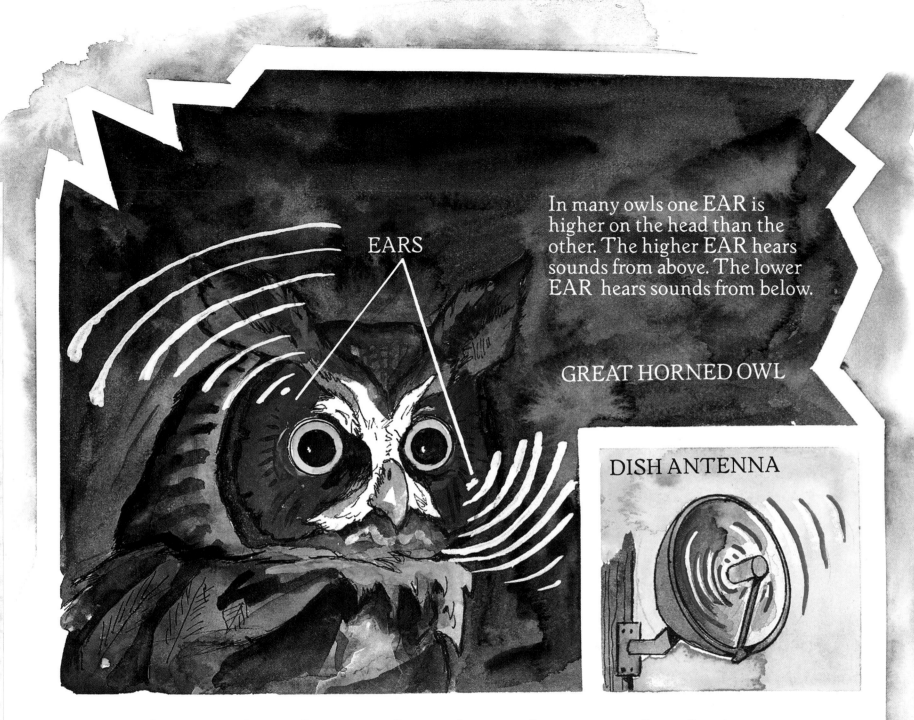

EARS

In many owls one EAR is higher on the head than the other. The higher EAR hears sounds from above. The lower EAR hears sounds from below.

GREAT HORNED OWL

DISH ANTENNA

Most owls rely on their keen hearing for hunting rather than their excellent vision. Their ears are hidden behind their facial disk feathers. These disks act like dish antennas to funnel sound to their ears. Owls are constantly turning their heads to hear better.

GREAT GRAY OWL

An owl attacks its prey silently. When flying, it can move its wings without making a sound. Silence...

An owl's bones are very light. They are full of air. The strength of an owl's wings and the lightness of its bones give an owl extraordinary lifting power.

Strong legs and toes, and long, needle-sharp curved talons give owls great grasping power. Most owls kill their prey by biting it at the base of the neck.

BARRED OWL

GREAT HORNED OWL

Different owls have different diets. They may eat squirrels, skunks, rabbits, birds, snakes, insects, and other creatures. Owls usually swallow their food whole, head first. When an owl kills an animal that is too big to swallow whole, it shreds it with its beak.

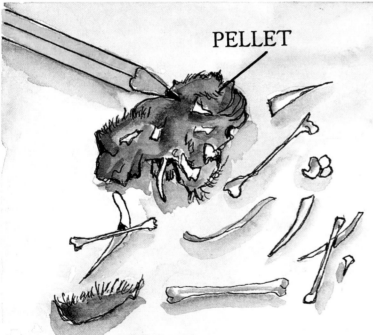

PELLET

Scientists study PELLETS to learn the food that different kinds of owls eat.

Owls cannot chew or grind their food. They cough up what they can't digest in pellets. The pellets usually contain fur and bones.

ELF OWL

GREAT HORNED OWL

Many owls rest, or roost, during the day. Some owls nap from time to time, resting their heads on their chests. Other owls twist their heads around to rest them on their backs.

BARRED OWL

"HOO-HOO-HOOHOO-AWWW"

SNOWY OWL

"KROW-OW"

BOREAL OWL

"TING-TING-TING"

GREAT HORNED OWL

"HOO-HOO-OO"

"HOOT! HOOT!" "SCREECH! SCREECH!"

Owls communicate in many ways. They may use sounds to claim a territory, to warn of danger, or call to a mate. Some people think owl sounds are eerie.

EASTERN SCREECH OWL

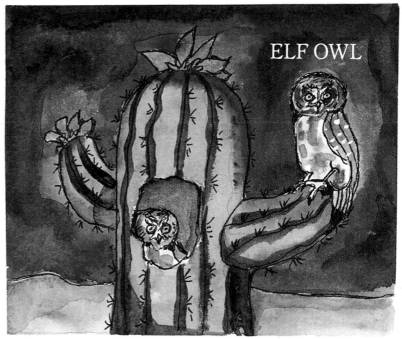

ELF OWL

GREAT GRAY OWL

Owls make nesting sites in unusual places. They may nest in hollow trees, in tree stumps, on the ground, or in abandoned birds' nests.

Many owls mate for life.

When a male barn owl courts a female barn owl, he will bring food to her as an offering. Often he flutters his powerful wings and hovers over her to get her attention. The male's mating call is "crooh-crooh."

When the female accepts the male, they mate. Then they choose a nesting site for the female to lay her eggs. Often they choose an old barn hayloft. Barn owls don't build nests. They use a space that is dark and safe.

EGG

Barn owls can lay
two to eleven eggs.

INCUBATION (in·kew·BAY·shun)
means keeping an egg warm
while a chick grows inside its shell.

A group of eggs is
called a CLUTCH.

In about two weeks the female begins laying her eggs.
She lays one egg at a time every two days. At the end of
ten days there are five eggs. She sits on them, keeping
them warm. This is called incubation.

EGG TOOTH

The barn owlet may weigh only ¾ ounce (21 grams).

A baby owl is called an OWLET.

About one month later, the female hears a faint peep coming from one of the eggs. The shell begins to crack. The first owlet uses its egg tooth to break free from the shell. The tiny owl is blind and helpless and has no feathers, but it can hear all the sounds around it. The male has been hunting, bringing food to its mate.

DOWN is soft feathers.

A group of owlets cared for together is called a BROOD.

At two weeks old the owlets can swallow their food whole.

Two days later the next owlet hatches. The mother keeps them warm and protects them with her soft feathers. At two weeks old the owlets can see. They are covered with soft down. Now both parents must hunt to feed their hungry brood.

Now the owlets are one month old. They have their feathers. Their eyesight is good. The owlets are very active and jump on the food their parents bring. They try flying.

When the owlets are two months old, they have moved outside of the barn and are able to fly. But they still need their parents to help them get food. When the young owls are about five months old, they are able to live on their own.

Chemicals weakened the eggshells of owls, so not as many owlets survived.

Years ago, there were many more owls in the world than there are today. People killed owls to protect smaller livestock. Farmers and others used chemicals to protect crops, plants, and trees from insects. Also, natural habitats were destroyed as people moved into wilderness areas.

ENDANGERED means in danger of no longer existing.

SPOTTED OWL

WILDLIFE RESERVE

When the owls are old enough, they are released back into their natural environments.

Today certain places have been set aside as reserves to protect owls. Some zoos have breeding programs for endangered owls. Owls play an important role in the balance of our natural world.

People don't see owls very often. That's because most owls are creatures of the night. When you are out in the country at night, listen carefully! You might hear the sound of an owl. "**HOoooo . . . HOoooo . . .**"

HOOT! HOOT! HOOT!

Scientists believe owls have been around for about 65 million years.

The Greek goddess Athena sometimes kept a small owl on her shoulder. She was the Greek goddess of wisdom. Perhaps that's how the saying "Wise as an owl" began.

A large owl in the wild can live to be 30 years old. In a zoo, where it is protected, an owl can live to be 60 years old.

Large owls live longer than small owls.

The burrowing owl can protect its burrow by making the sound of a rattlesnake.

The barn owl has the best hearing of all owls. It can hear a mouse's footsteps 90 feet (2700 cm) away. Barn owls are sometimes called "monkey faced."

The snowy owl has feathers on its feet so it won't get frostbite.

It is hard to spot owls in the wild during the day. Their feathers camouflage them. That means they blend in with their surroundings.

A group of owls is called a parliament.

People who stay out late at night are called "night owls."